Environment Sweden

U.S. Environmental Protection Agency

The BiblioGov Project is an effort to expand awareness of the public documents and records of the U.S. Government via print publications. In broadening the public understanding of government and its work, an enlightened democracy can grow and prosper. Ranging from historic Congressional Bills to the most recent Budget of the United States Government, the BiblioGov Project spans a wealth of government information. These works are now made available through an environmentally friendly, print-on-demand basis, using only what is necessary to meet the required demands of an interested public. We invite you to learn of the records of the U.S. Government, heightening the knowledge and debate that can lead from such publications.

Included are the following Collections:

Budget of The United States Government	Code of Federal Regulations
Presidential Documents	Congressional Documents
United States Code	Economic Indicators
Education Reports from ERIC	Federal Register
GAO Reports	Government Manuals
History of Bills	House Journal
House Rules and Manual	Privacy act Issuances
Public and Private Laws	Statutes at Large

OCLC11859214

ENVIRONMENT

SWEDEN

Office of International Activities
U.S. Environmental Protection Agency
January 1977

E
 N
  V
   I
    R
     O
      N
       M
        E
         N
          T

S
 W
  E
   D
    E
     N

Office of International Activities
Environmental Protection Agency
January 1977

PREFACE

This is a brief report on the organization and management of environmental activities on the national level in Sweden. Reports on Japan, Luxemburg, Belgium, Great Britain, the Netherlands, Spain, Australia and the Federal Republic of Germany have already been distributed. Similar reports on other countries will be available soon. These reports, which are background papers for EPA staff involved in international activities, are not for distribution outside the Agency.

Emphasis is on policy and regulatory functions of national environmental agencies as well as on legal instruments for environmental control. Research and development, often under the auspices of other departments, for example, science and technology, are not covered in these reports.

Source documents for the reports, received under the International Documents Exchange, are available in the EPA Headquarters Library. English summaries of the foreign documents are published in the monthly bulletin "Summaries of Foreign Government Reports."

TABLE OF CONTENTS

E N V I R O N M E N T A L   C O N T R O L   I N   S W E D E N

I.   ## National Organization for Environmental Control

overall government structure

Sweden is a constitutional monarchy governed under democratic and
parliamentary principles. The new constitution, effective January 1, 1975,
assigns to the King, as head of state, purely symbolic functions, while vesting
executive authority in the Prime Minister as head of government and the cabinet
of ministers (Regeringen – Government). Decisions of government are no longer
signed by the King. The new constitution specifies that the speaker of parliament,
after consultation within parliament, is to nominate the prime ministerial candi-
date, who must be confirmed by majority vote. The Prime Minister lists candidates
for his Cabinet.

While legislative authority in Sweden rests with the unicameral parliament, or Riksdag, proportionally elected by universal suffrage, the Cabinet governs
the country, as provided in the Instrument of Government. The Cabinet is accountable
to the Riksdag.

The Prime Minister can be removed from office at his own request, by the
Speaker of the Riksdag, or in the event of a vote of no confidence in the Riksdag.
Other ministers can be removed at their own request, by the Prime Minister, or by
means of a no confidence vote. Should the Prime Minister leave office through
resignation or death, all ministers of his Cabinet must tender their resignations.

The ministries formulate policy and issue clarifying ordinances. They
are, however, relatively small bodies, and the actual implementation of policy is
carried out by a number of boards or agencies, staffed by civil servants, with
specialized areas of competence, such as the National Environment Protection
Board. Although jurisdictionally subordinate to the ministries, these boards

-1-

have independent authority to make decisions implementing policy.

Sweden has an independent judiciary with justices appointed for life by the Cabinet. To protect the public interest, three ombudsmen (Justitieombudsmän), appointed by parliament for four-year terms, provide an independent check on the court, military and administrative systems, with the exclusion of the Cabinet.

national environmental agency

The Ministry of Agriculture (Jordbruksdepartementet) is responsible for formation of environmental policy and is the source of proposals for environmental legislation and budget. Since 1968, an Environmental Advisory Committee, chaired by the Minister of Agriculture and composed of representatives of the scientific community, industry, and both national and municipal governments, has functioned within the ministry to provide expert advice and information to the Government.

The National Environment Protection Board (Statens naturvårdsverk - SNV), subordinate to the Ministry of Agriculture, is Sweden's central administrative authority for environmental control. Duties of the Board, established in 1967, have gradually expanded to include almost all aspects of environmental protection with the exception of radiation control. (See organizational chart, page 2a.)

Currently the National Environment Protection Board (SNV) is responsible for the planning, coordination, supervision, and enforcement of measures relating to air and water pollution control, noise abatement, solid waste management, and control of products hazardous to health and to the environment. SNV coordinates and promotes environmental research and administers research grants for and grants for municipal sewage purification plants and pollution control measures in industry. It a coordinates and provides advice and assistance to regional and local governmental bodies responsible for environmental affairs. In addition, it is entrusted with preservation of the natural environment and wildlife as well as with support to outdoor recreation and sports.

-2-

NATIONAL ENVIRONMENT PROTECTION BOARD
(Statens naturvårdsverk)

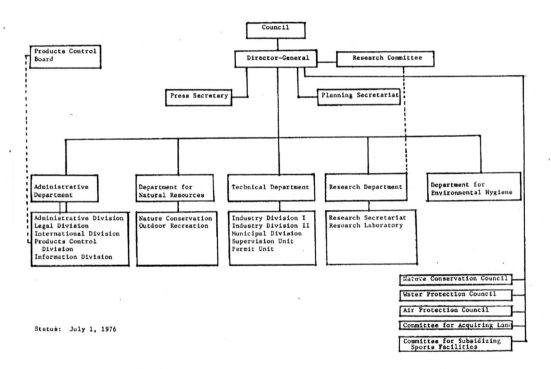

Status: July 1, 1976

SNV is headed by the Director General, appointed by the Cabinet to serve for six years, and by the Council, composed of the Director General, up to six other members, appointed by the Cabinet for three-year terms, and two SNV employee representatives. SNV employs approximately 600 persons.

Since July 1976, SNV has been organized into the following major sections: the Administrative, Natural Resources, Technical, and Research Departments, the Planning Secretariat, and the Environmental Hygiene Department.[1]* Serving in an advisory capacity to SNV are various councils and committees, including the councils for Nature Conservation, Water Protection, and Air Protection, and the Committee for Acquiring Land.[2] The Research Committee has both advisory and decision-making functions, the latter primarily in regard to the allocation of SNV research grants.[3] Members are appointed to these groups by the Cabinet on the basis of their specialized knowledge and are charged with keeping abreast of current developments in their areas. They represent the administrative authorities, organizations and research institutes that are particularly concerned with environmental matters.

The Administrative Department includes the Administrative, Legal, International, and Information Divisions. It also includes the Products Control Division,[4] which is involved in implementing the environmental aspects of legislation on products hazardous to health and the environment and which serves as the executive body for the Products Control Board. In the Technical Department, two Industrial Divisions and a Municipal Division administer matters relating to air and water conservation and noise abatement, particularly with regard to environmental protection legislation. They are responsible too for remaining abreast of and reporting technical progress in these areas. The department is involved in matters relating to state grants for sewage purification plants and for environmental protection in industry. Also in this department is the unit which examines applications for exemptions to the

*All reference notes will be found beginning on page 27.

-3-

requirement of the 1969 Environment Protection Act that certain potentially polluting establishments obtain permits to begin or continue operations.[5]

The Research Department includes the Research Laboratory and the Research Secretariat. The Research Laboratory analyzes water and air samples and conducts other investigations to assist SNV in its inventory, planning, exemption, and monitoring functions. It also develops measurement methodology.[6] The Research Secretariat observes environmental research at home and abroad and disseminates information. It serves as an executive and advisory adjunct to the Research Committee, in which capacity it processes applications for research grants.[7] The Research Committee itself coordinates research in the natural and environmental areas, makes certain that the research has practical significance, and allocates research grants.[8]

The Environmental Hygiene Department, which is closely affiliated with the Royal Caroline Institute in Stockholm, studies the effects of air, water and noise pollution on health and directs courses for public health inspectors and water examiners.[9]

In Sweden, environmental protection includes conservation of nature and wildlife, maintenance of nature reserves and parks and support to outdoor recreational activities. These matters are dealt with by the Natural Resources Department. The Committee for Subsidizing Sports Activities acts in an advisory capacity in certain of these areas.

The Planning Secretariat is responsible for general planning and coordination within SNV, especially across division lines.[10] It is also involved in the comprehensive national physical planning work now in progress.

other agencies with major responsibilities in environment

In addition to SNV, two other agencies subordinate to the Ministry of Agriculture, the National Franchise Board for Environment Protection (Koncessions-

-4-

nämnden för miljöskydd) and the Products Control Board (Produktkontrollnämnden),
have specialized environmental functions.

The National Franchise Board for Environment Protection deals with applications from industry and local authorities for permits to pollute under provisions of the 1969 Environment Protection Act. Although it is an administrative body, this Board functions somewhat like a court of law. It consists of a president with legal and judicial experience and three other members: a technical expert, an expert in environmental affairs, and a member with either industrial or municipal experience, depending on the case being heard.

The Products Control Board is administratively linked with SNV, whose Director General acts as its chairman. Created to implement the 1973 Act on Products Hazardous to Health and to the Environment, it promulgates regulations on the manufacture, handling, importation and marketing of hazardous products, such as poisons, pesticides, and PCBs (polychlorinated biphenyls). It further directs, coordinates and broadly monitors all other aspects of product control. This includes considering applications for registration of pesticides and for permits to import, handle, sell, transfer or use commercially certain PCBs. The Board also conducts surveys and investigations of products suspected of being hazardous to health or to the environment. However, routine supervision to ensure that product control laws and regulations are being observed is left to SNV and to the National Board of Industrial Safety within their respective spheres of activity.

Certain environmental functions fall within the jurisdiction of several other agencies. For example, the National Institute of Radiation Protection is the central authority regulating the use of radioactive substances and their emissions. The Board of Customs and its coastguard service are responsible for the control of oil pollution in coastal waters. The National Board of Shipping and Navigation has installations at six major and 22 smaller ports where for a fee ships may dispose of oil residues and oil-polluted water rather than discharging them into the sea. The National Road Administration and the National Road Safety Board handle certain matters pertaining to air pollution from motor vehicles. The National Board of Health and Welfare deals with air, water and noise pollution in accordance with public health and radiation protection legislation. The National Board of Urban Planning is involved in some phases of physical planning and land use which are important from an environmental standpoint. Finally, an office within the Ministry for Foreign Affairs in cooperation with the Swedish Institute disseminates information at the international level.[11]

national-regional-local government relationships

Sweden has a unitary system of government under which major laws and regulations are formulated at the national level and implemented fairly uniformly by successive levels of regional and local government.

There are 24 counties (län), which are constitutionally subordinate to the national government. Each is governed by a county administration board (länsstyrelse) composed of the governor and ten other members. The governor and five other board members are cabinet appointees and, as such, represent a direct line of communication with the national government. The remaining five board members are appointed by the popularly elected county council (landsting), the regional legislative entity which deals with health and education matters. Counties are subdivided into municipalities (kommun), which are governed by elected municipal councils (kommunfullmäktige).

Swedish environmental administration is characterized by a centralized national environmental policy and a decentralized implementation of policy. Although SNV exercises central administrative control in the environmental area, the environment protection and nature conservancy sections of county administrations carry out the continuous, direct implementation of national environmental regulations, acting in this respect as the regional arm of the national government. Municipal authorities cooperate and exchange information with the national and county jurisdictions, but they deal with aspects of environmental control that are of purely local character in that national law makes them responsible for application of health and sanitation laws.

County administration authorities are specifically charged with ensuring observation of environmental law, issuing directives, and employing persuasive or, if necessary, coercive means to achieve compliance. They are authorized to consider some applications for exemption from the obligation to apply to the National Franchise Board for a permit to begin or continue a polluting activity. County authorities monitor for adherence to conditions of all permits and exemptions by facilities within their jurisdictions. They also have considerable responsibility under nature conservancy laws and enforce on a regional basis controls on products hazardous to health and to the environment.

Municipal authorities may issue their own local bylaws in implementing national health and sanitation legislation. Public health committees ensure that measures are taken to check or counteract air and water pollution and other nuisances insofar as they constitute threats to human health and well-being. Most action against particular sources of noise is taken at the municipal level. Moreover, municipal authorities bear complete responsibility for the collection and disposal of domestic and some industrial refuse, accomplished through contracts with private firms. Local building committees take environmental needs into consideration during urban planning, and current national physical planning programs call for municipalities to implement guidelines in this area established by the Riksdag in 1972.[12]

County and municipal authorities also see to the removal of oil on beaches and oil spills on shore.[13]

II. Environmental Laws

legislative system

The Riksdag, Sweden's unicameral legislative body, consists of 349
seats. Members are elected for three-year terms, 310 from 28 constituencies,
and the remainder from a national pool to ensure proportional representation
of majority parties.

The Riksdag alone exercises the powers of taxation and appropriation,
but it shares with the Cabinet the power to legislate by regulation or decree
certain areas of civil and criminal law. Although legislation may be initiated
by the Cabinet or Riksdag deputies, most major policy proposals originate in
the Cabinet. After discussion in the Riksdag, proposals are sent to numerous
standing or special committees, where a major portion of the work on a bill is
accomplished. Bills reported out of committee, together with any counter-
proposals, are voted upon in the plenary Riksdag. After passage, requiring
three readings, bills are sent to the Cabinet for signature by the appropriate
minister and subsequent promulgation.

Modern Swedish legislation, especially that pertaining to technically
complex subjects like pollution control, tends to be a three-tiered effort,
consisting of a generally worded framework law, a more specific clarifying ordinance issued by a ministry, and concrete administrative guidelines from an agency.[14]

highlights of environmental laws

comprehensive environmental law

The May 29, 1969 Environment Protection Act and the pursuant Environment
Protection Ordinance constitute comprehensive legislation to control or prevent
air and water pollution and disturbances due to noise, vibration or light.
Specifically the Act applies to: 1) discharge of wastewater, solids or gas

from land, buildings or installations into a watercourse, lake or other area of water, 2) use of land, buildings or installations so as to cause pollution of water, and 3) use of land, buildings or installations leading to interference with the environment through air pollution, noise, vibration or light if the disturbance is other than temporary. The Act does not apply to the effects of ionizing radiation.

It is important to note that the Act is limited to the control of pollution arising from the use of real estate. Pollution resulting from the use of a road or an airport may be regulated under the Act only insofar as precautions relate to the use of the fixed installation, but disturbances from motor vehicles, aircraft and ships are subject to other legislation, as are obstructions to the flow of water and constructions in water.

The Act stipulates that an entrepreneur must choose the location of his facility and take any technologically and economically feasible precautionary measures in order to minimize adverse environmental effects. It establishes a permit system, specifying that before certain types of establishments may be constructed, or certain wastewaters discharged, permission must be obtained from the National Franchise Board for Environment Protection. Alternately, an exemption from the permit requirement may be obtained from the National Environment Protection Board (SNV) or, in some instances, from the relevant county administration. In the case of other specified types of establishments regarded as less polluting, an entrepreneur need not obtain a permit, but must merely notify SNV or county authorities well in advance of commencing operation. The Act authorizes prohibition of a potentially polluting activity if it is judged that no reasonable precaution will adequately protect the environment.

A change in the structure or in the use of an installation is subject to terms of the Act if it can bring about increased pollution or a change in the composition of pollution or in the manner in which pollutants are discharged. Plants existing when the Act took effect are usually required to meet less stringent requirements initially and are given longer periods of time to achieve compliance than new facilities. The mere risk of nuisance is sufficient to call provisions of the Act into effect.

Any potentially polluting establishment _may_ apply for a permit, but certain types of installations _must_ apply. The Environment Protection Ordinance specifies 38 types of facilities requiring permission to begin or continue polluting, 25 kinds of installations subject to notification requirements, and the types o wastewater subject to control. Industrial, agricultural and municipal installations are all subject to control by this legislation.

Another piece of legislation containing general provisions relative to pollution problems is the December 19, 1958 Public Health Statute, as amended. It charges municipal public health committees with enforcing measures against air and water pollution, noise and other nuisances at the local level. Regulations pertaining to dumps, sewage and industrial facilities are included in the Statute.

water pollution legislation

The Water Code of June 28, 1918, as amended, includes regulations governing construction in water, obstructions to the flow of water, changes in water level, and protection of underground water. Before construction may occur, permission must be granted by a Water Rights Court. Because solids tipped into a body of water alter water level, prior permission from county authorities is required. In some instances overlap may occur with the Environment Protection Act, and an entrepreneur might require permission under both laws.[15] The April 29, 1964 Law to Amend the Water Code, which contains specific provisions for protection of groundwater resources, empowers authorities to establish protective zones around sources of groundwater and issue regulations pertinent to these zones.

The December 17, 1971 Marine Dumping Prohibition Act, proscribes the discharge of any solid, liquid or gaseous waste into Swedish territorial waters from a ship or other means of transport. No Swedish vessel may dump such waste into the open sea, nor is waste to be transported from Sweden in any nations's vessel with the intention of dumping at sea. The pursuant ordinance provides that the National Environment Protection Board may grant exemption from these requirements if it is manifest that no detriment to the environment will result.

A number of measures to control oil discharges from ships on the high seas or in port are contained in the June 2, 1972 Act Concerning Prevention of Water Pollution From Ships, as amended. Swedish shippers may be required to verify compliance with construction or equipment standards and to maintain oil record books. Authorities may issue regulations preventing foreign vessels from putting in at Swedish ports or using Swedish-controlled loading and discharge stations at sea without certificates attesting to structural features. The Act further authorizes regulation of the discharge of other polluting matter originating in a ship's operation.

The January 22, 1976 Act No. 6 on Measures Against Water Pollution From Ships Within the Baltic Area contains provisions pertaining to oil, toilet, solid and certain other wastes. It authorizes the Government or an authority designated by the Government to issue guidelines on the handling of such wastes and to forbid the loading of oil, repair of ships or other activities that could cause oil pollution if oil-receiving or water treatment stations are not available. The June 17, 1976 Ordinance pursuant to this law delineates those instances in which authorities are to issue regulations. All such regulations must conform to provisions of the Baltic Convention.

air pollution legislation

Motor vehicles and sulfur emissions from heating facilities account for a significant portion of urban air pollution. Specific legislation deals with these problems.

The November 20, 1968 Statutory Regulation on Reduction of Sulfur Content in Fuel Oil establishes the maximum permissible sulfur content by weight in heating oil. It allows local public health authorities to set more stringent standards in high pollution areas or to allow use of lower grade fuel if emissions are effectively treated. The March 24, 1972 Statutory Regulation on Reduction of Sulfur Content in Fuel Oil amends the 1968 statute to decrease the maximum permissible content by weight in fuel oils used in certain metropolitan areas.

Authority to control pollution caused by motor vehicles is contained in the December 1, 1972 Ordinance on Vehicle Exhaust Emissions,[16] which prescribes that a vehicle with an internal combustion engine, if gasoline-driven, must have closed crankcase ventilation and an effective device to limit exhaust emissions. It delineates increasingly stringent standards to reduce emitted carbon monoxide, hydrocarbons, and nitrogen oxides. The regulations apply to vehicles with a gross weight under 2.5 metric tons equipped with an engine having a cylinder volume of at least 0.8 liters or producing over 30 horsepower. The ordinance sets standards for the opacity of emissions from diesel-powered vehicles and requires such vehicles to have sealed fuel injection pumps.

other program areas

The March 14, 1958 Statute on Protection Against Radiation, as amended, controls dangers from ionizing radiation. It makes any "radiological work" (defined as an endeavor involving radioactive substances, nuclear energy, X-ray equipment or other device which emits ionizing radiation) subject to a permit from the National Institute of Radiation Protection and specifies conditions under which a

-12-

permit may be granted. Requirements for supervision and inspection of facilities engaged in work with radioactive substances are established.

The April 27, 1973 Act on Products Hazardous to Health and to the Environment and the pursuant Ordinance state rules for manufacturing, handling, importing, and marketing products, including poisons, pesticides, PCBs and PCB products, which may involve risks due to their chemical or physico-chemical properties.

The December 17, 1970 Statute on Cleanliness in the Municipalities, as amended, makes municipal authorities responsible for collection and environmentally compatible disposal of household and some industrial refuse. Municipal authorities · must maintain sanitary conditions of streets, squares, parks, and other public places and are ultimately responsible for removal of litter and restoration of deteriorated places, though they may seek restitution from the polluter. The December 13, 1974 Royal Ordinance on Sanitation, passed pursuant to the 1970 law, requires local author- ities to consider health and environmental aspects when planning the collection of dirt and refuse.

Sections 23 and 24 of the 1964 Law for the Protection of Nature, as amended, prohibit the disposal of sheet metal, glass, plastic, paper or waste in such a manner as to cause deterioration of the environment.

Special provisions for the disposal of specified solid and liquid chemical wastes are contained in the May 22, 1975 Ordinance on Environmentally Dangerous Wastes. It provides regulations pertaining to the reporting, permission for transportation, final disposal, import and supervision of such wastes.

Finally, the May 22, 1975 Automobile Scrapping Law and pursuant Ordinance provide for the environmentally compatible disposal of used automobiles.

Noise abatement regulations are found in traffic and aviation laws and in local building and health codes in addition to the stipulations of the Environment Protection Act. Noise from traffic and other sources may also be controlled in the

-13-

course of urban planning.

Laws important in current programs of physical and land use planning include the <u>1947 Building Act</u>, the <u>1959 Building Statute</u>, and the <u>1964 Law for the Protection of Nature</u>.

promulgation

National laws are published chronologically as they appear in <u>Svensk författningssamling</u>, the official Swedish legal gazette. They are systematically compiled on a yearly basis in the privately published, but officially recognized, <u>Sveriges rikes lag</u>.

III.   Status of Air and Water Standards

general

Standards for the sulfur content of fuel oil, motor vehicle exhaust emissions, and the lead content of gasoline have been established by law. Compulsory national ambient quality and pollutant discharge levels for air and water have not been established. Instead SNV publishes recommended guidelines on the basis of which examining authorities set legally binding standards case by case to meet the needs of individual establishments when issuing permits or exemption certificates.

water standards

Although no legal water standards exist, generally acceptable informal guidelines for judging water quality have been evolved during nearly a century's tradition of examination of receiving waters in Sweden. In 1969, SNV published suggested surface water criteria for public water supplies, bathing areas and water suitable for fish, as well as suggested criteria for identifying waters as unpolluted, slightly polluted, distinctly polluted and heavily polluted, taking into account physical, chemical, and bacteriological factors.[17] Suggested physical parameters for classifying waters as slightly to heavily polluted include: a temperature increase of from 1°C to 5°C; a distinct to strong taste and odor increase; a color increase of from 10 to 100 percent; and a turbidity increase of from two to twenty ppm silicon dioxide (SiO_2). Suggested chemical criteria span the following ranges: an oxygen saturation change of from 10 to 50 percent; a permanganate consumption increase of from 10 to 100 percent (or 5 to 50 ppm potassium permanganate - $KMnO_4$); a biological oxygen demand (BOD_7) increase of from 1 to 6 ppm; an alkalinity decrease of 10 to 50 percent (or pH less than 5.5); an alkalinity increase of from 10 to 100 percent (or pH greater than 9);

-15-

an electric conductivity increase of from 10 to 100 percent; an iron increase of from 0.1 to 1.0 ppm; a manganese increase of from 0.02 to 0.20 ppm; and total phosphorous increase of from 20 to 100 percent.[18] SNV has stated that it will decide whether or not to set official standards after considerable experience with these criteria.[19]

air standards

The November 28, 1968 Statutory Regulation on Reduction of Sulfur Content in Fuel Oil establishes the maximum permissible content of sulfur in heating oil at 2.5 percent by weight, while the March 24, 1972 Statutory Regulation on Reduction of Sulfur Content in Fuel Oil sets a maximum fuel oil sulfur content of one percent by weight for use in the urban areas of Stockholm, Gothenburg, Malmo, Lund and Jönköping.

With regard to air pollution from mobile sources, the December 1, 1972 Ordinance on Vehicle Exhaust Emissions adopts United States exhaust emissions standards for 1973 model automobiles for 1976 model Swedish vehicles, stipulating that per kilometer exhaust gases may not contain more than 24.2 grams carbon monoxide, 2.1 grams hydrocarbons, and 1.9 grams nitrogen oxides. For vehicles manufactured from 1971 through 1975, standards of 45 grams carbon monoxide and 2.2 grams hydrocarbons per kilometer apply. Carbon monoxide emissions from 1970 and earlier model vehicles are not to exceed 4.5 percent of total emissions by volume while the vehicle is idling and in a state of good repair. The Ordinance also stipulated that diesel-powered buses designed for more than 30 passengers may not register a smoke density of more than 2.5 measured on a Bosch instrument Type EFAW-68, or 30 units measured on a Hartridge instrument. Smoke density in other diesel-driven vehicles should not exceed 3.5 on a Bosch instrument or 45 on a Hartridge instrument.

A regulation of January 28, 1969 establishes the maximum lead content of gasoline at 0.7 grams per liter, starting in 1970. This value was to be reduced to 0.4 grams per liter effective January 1973 and to 0.15 grams per liter effective January 1976.[20] However, in 1973, the Environment Protection Board decided to prolong observance of the 0.7 gram lead maximum due to the energy shortage.[21]

For the control of pollution from industrial enterprises, SNV has published technical guidelines giving recommended maximum emission levels for certain pollutants from various stationary sources. These guidelines, not compulsory in themselves, reflect what can normally be expected from a plant of a given sort under current technological and economic conditions. Although only those standards set for an individual installation by an examining authority in a permit or an exemption certificate are legally binding, emission limits specified in permits have in the past usually corresponded closely to guideline levels.[22]

Technical emissions guidelines exist for the following types of stationary sources: iron and steel works; ferro-alloy plants; sintering plants; foundries; copper and aluminum melting works; surface treatment plants; cement works; stone crushing plants; plants producing lime or lime products; asphalt works; petroleum refineries; petroleum product storage depots; sulfuric acid, chlor-alkali, sulfate-cellulose, and sulphite-cellulose factories; heavy oil heating plants with a capacity over 50 megawatts for producing heat or steam; gas turbine power stations; waste incineration installations; wood or bark burning installations, and cable scrap incineration installations.[23] There are also guidelines for stack height calculation and for measurement and evaluation of emissions levels. Emissions levels stipulated in guidelines refer to the average total discharge during a specified period of time, usually one month.

-17-

The National Environment Protection Board has issued ambient air quality standards for sulfur dioxide and for smoke. Both maximum standards and short-term standards are stated for sulfur dioxide. During the winter months (October to March), the average maximum concentration of sulfur dioxide in the air is not to exceed 100 micrograms per cubic meter. For a 24-hour period, the average maximum concentration is not to exceed 300 micrograms per cubic meter for more than three inconsecutive days. (This is equal to two percent of the time.) For one hour, the maximum concentration is not to exceed 750 micrograms per cubic meter more than one percent of the time during one month. The long-term goal for the winter season is a maximum concentration of no more than 60 micrograms per cubic meter. In 24 hours, the long-term goal is established at 200 micrograms per cubic meter, not to be exceeded for more than three inconsecutive days.

Standards for smoke stipulate a maximum concentration of 40 micrograms per cubic meter during the winter season. For a 24-hour period, the maximum concentration is not to exceed 120 micrograms per cubic meter during more than three inconsecutive days.

For total particulate matter, the American standards for particulates are recommended as a guideline.[24]

promulgation

Standards issued as parts of regulations are promulgated in the official legal gazette, Svensk författningssamling. Recommended criteria and technical guidelines are contained in separate publications of the National Environment Protection Board.[25] SNV establishes recommended air and water standards on the basis of reports submitted by specially appointed working groups.[26]

IV.   Enforcement Procedures

court system

In Sweden there are 100 district courts (tingsrätt), six courts of appeal (hovrätt), and the Supreme Court (högsta domstol). The district courts hear both civil and criminal cases. For a criminal case, the court consists of a professional judge and five elected lay judges. In civil cases, the court usually consists of three professional judges. Appellate courts are composed of a president, judges of appeal and assessors. The Supreme Court, the court of highest appeal, has 23 members and works in divisions of five members each, although some cases may be heard by full session of the court.

A separate system of administrative courts exists. In each of the 24 counties, there is a County Administrative Court (länsrätt) and a County Fiscal Court (länsskatterätt). Decisions may be appealed to one of the two Administrative Courts of Appeal (kammarrätt), or finally, to the Supreme Administrative Court (regeringsrätt).

Certain special courts such as the real estate courts (fastighets-domstolar) and the water rights courts (vattendomstolar), which are usually specialized district courts, are important in implementation of environmental legislation. A district court functioning as a real estate court consists of two judges, a technological expert and two lay assessors.[27]

enforcement mechanisms and procedures

Enforcement mechanisms provided for in the Environment Protection Act include the powers of supervisory authorities, the permit system, and monetary compensation or compulsory purchase of property for individuals suffering hardship as a result of polluting activities.

Permits are issued to polluting establishments by the National Franchise

Board after a thorough, formal investigation, usually lasting about a year.
They have the legal force of the decision of a court of law for a stipulated
time period, usually ten years. On the other hand, an exemption certificate is issued by the National Environment Protection Board or by a county administration after
a comprehensive, but less formal, negotiatory procedure averaging three months.
The exemption binds the holder to its provisions, but it does not have the legal
validity of a permit, so that theoretically another authority might impose more
stringent requirements on the holder. This rarely happens in practice, since
all interested authorities are consulted during the investigation. There is
no appeal from an exemption decision, but decisions of the Franchise Board
may be appealed to the Ministry of Agriculture.

Although SNV is ultimately responsible for enforcement of terms
of the Environment Protection Act, county administration officials carry out
routine enforcement of its provisions. Supervisory agencies are charged with
an active, casefinding role in locating and correcting sources of pollution.
Enforcement authorities first seek voluntary cooperation by polluters, but
they also have various tools of coercion at their disposal.

SNV may refer a case to the Franchise Board, which may prohibit
an activity or prescribe control measures if a permit has not been issued.
County administration authorities may intervene directly, issuing injunctions
or instructions in clear cases of violation. If a permit or exemption is being
violated, the county administration may order the holder to rectify the situa-
tion, under threat of financial penalty if necessary, or steps may be taken
to correct the matter at the permit holder's expense.

In exercising their duties, enforcement officials have the right of
access to property and the right to carry out any investigations. The property

owner is obliged to provide the examining authority with required information.

Individual citizens have various channels of recourse in the face of a polluting activity. They may demand compensation for damage due to pollution arising from negligence, and, even if negligence cannot be shown, they may receive compensation if the pollution is found to be unreasonable in the view of local conditions or of what is usual in other places under similar circumstances. Claims for compensation are made at a district real estate court. If a property owner believes his property's usefulness is severely impaired by pollution, he may sue for compulsory purchase by the polluter of all or parts of the property. An individual may also demand that the court issue an injunction or specify limitations to a polluting activity. Citizens or public authorities may further report cases of pollution to SNV or county administration officials, who must inform the complainant whether or not action is to be taken.[28]

Public health regulations are enforced at the municipal level by public health committees. They offer advice and issue directives for the prevention or elimination of sanitary nuisances, and if the advice and directives are ignored, they may issue injunctions and prohibitions, with monetary penalties attached. Decisions of public health committees may be appealed to county administration officials.

Compliance with the Marine Dumping Prohibition Act is ensured by county administration officials in cooperation with local customs authorities. National supervision is the responsibility of SNV in consultation with the Board of Customs. Supervisory authorities may board any means of transport, enter premises used in connection with dumping, make examinations, and demand necessary information.

penalties

Under the Environment Protection Act, a polluter may suffer fine or
imprisonment of up to one year for: 1) violating a prohibition issued by the
Franchise Board, 2) beginning work on an activity subject to permission without
having obtained the necessary permit or exemption, 3) beginning work which must be
reported to authorities in advance without having done so, or 4) disregarding the te:
or conditions of a permit or exemption. Penal liability is based on the offender's
having acted willfully or negligently. Legal proceedings for these infringe-
ments are conducted at an ordinary court of law.[29] In cases of serious violation
of a permit, the Franchise Board may annul the permit and prohibit further activity.

For violation of a provision of the Marine Dumping Act, persons are
liable to fine or imprisonment up to one year. Property used to commit an
offense, or an equivalent value, may be declared forfeit.

Failure of a ship owner or his delegated representative to keep an
oil record book in accordance with the Act Concerning Prevention of Water Pollution from Ships may result in a fine or imprisonment of up to six months.

A fine of up to 500 Swedish kronor may be levied against anyone opera-
ting a vehicle contrary to provisions of the Ordinance on Vehicle Exhaust Emissions.

V. Interrelationships Between Government and Industry

general

Industry and other interest areas have institutionalized roads
of access to the government policy-making process through royal commissions and
the remiss procedure. Royal commissions are investigative committees appointed
by the Cabinet or by an individual minister to study a specific issue and recom-
mend legislative action. Members of royal commissions are drawn in nearly equal
numbers from civil service, political parties, and interest groups, such as the
Swedish Federation of Industries. A royal commission, once appointed, works
independently of government control, although its final report is very often
accepted as the basis of the Government's policy proposal in the Riksdag.

The remiss procedure represents a process of consultation. Ministries
are constitutionally obligated to solicit opinions from relevant administrative
agencies prior to reaching final decisions on issues at cabinet level. Tradi-
tionally they also ask for interest group opinions on anticipated government measures. They then submit remiss opinions together with original documents and the
Government's recommendation to the Riksdag. The Swedish Federation of Industries
has been a major contributor of remiss opinions.[30] Representatives of industry
may also serve on government advisory committees or be appointed to the Councils
of administrative agencies. Routine consultation and exchange of information and
technical data occur between government officials and industrial representatives
of all levels.

polluter pays principle

Sweden subscribes to the theory that the polluter should pay the cost
of preventing or alleviating pollution. New industry must include pollution control costs in investment estimates from the outset.

To facilitate the adjustment of existing industry to new standards, the government provided a five-year system of grants through the 1969 Ordinance on State Subsidy to Anti-Pollution Measures in Industry. Up to 25 percent of investment costs for measures to limit air, water or noise pollution could be subsidized through June 30, 1974. An amendment extended the program through June 30, 1975. Government aid for measures to combat air, water, and noise pollution in agriculture is available until June 30, 1977 under the June 2, 1972 Ordinance No. 293. State subsidies for waste treatment facilities are authorized by the June 2, 1972 Ordinance 280. Finally, the April 26, 1968 Ordinance 308 on State Subsidy for Wastewater Purification Works allows grants of from 30 to 50 percent of costs to municipalities for purification greater than sludge separation, based on degree of purification.

During a period of recession in the early 1970's, the Government used increased grants to industry and to municipal wastewater purification plants to stimulate the economy while furthering protection of the environment. Between November 1, 1971 and June 30, 1972, it was possible for grants to industry to equal up to 75 percent of investment costs if work was begun and 60 percent completed during the period. From September 1, 1972 through April 30, 1973 and in November and December 1973, industry grants could total up to 50 percent of costs. Municipal sewage purification plants had access to increased grants of 55 to 75 percent of costs for the same periods.[31]

From 1960 to 1973, based on investment figures contained in applications for grants, the Swedish government subsidized about one-third of industrial investment for pollution control in established industries.[32]

major industries

Major economic endeavors in Sweden include construction, mining, quarrying, manufacturing, and provision of electricity, gas, water and sanitary services. Important branches of manufacturing include production of metals, metal products, machinery and transportation equipment. Also significant are the production of high quality and ordinary steel, the chemical and petrochemical industries, and the mining of iron ore. Because forests cover about 57 percent of Sweden's land area, forestry and forest-based industries, such as sawmills, plywood factories, joinery industries, pulp and paper mills, wallboard and particle board factories make important contributions to the economy.

industrial monitoring and inspection systems

Swedish environmental policy holds that supervision of polluting establishments by the authorities should merely provide a check on the plant's own control measures.[33] Therefore, SNV, in cooperation with representatives of industry, has drawn up standard programs describing how supervision is to be conducted at various types of installations, in accordance with the Environment Protection Act. Typically, a program of supervisory activities is worked out by the management of a particular plant and submitted to the county administration for approval. The program, which becomes part of the permit or exemption certificate, specifies what is required of the plant in the way of operational controls, monitoring and inspection programs, periodic checks and measurements, and the manner of reporting results.[34]

liaison practices

The National Environment Protection Board has adopted a policy of working closely with industry, feeling that cooperation facilitates industry's adoption of increasingly stringent requirements. For example, informal cooperation between government, representatives of the detergent industry, and scientists brought about an agreement by the industry to reduce the phosphate content of detergents sold in Sweden.[35] Mercury effluents were cut 95 percent in the alkali-chlorine industry after consultation with SNV and the Swedish Water and Air Pollution Laboratory (Institutet för Vatten- och Luftvårdsforskning).[36] The latter body is financed equally by government and industry so that problems may be treated adequately from both the public and private sector points of view.[37]

SNV frequently forms special joint committees or work groups composed of its own personnel and representatives of branches of industry to solve particular technical problems of pollution control. In 1969, work groups of this sort studied the air pollution problems in various branches of industry and submitted recommendations on which SNV based its 1969 guidelines for air emissions standards in industry. The standards were revised in 1973, again with the aid of industry.

Encouraged by both SNV and the Swedish Federation of Industries, many industries have appointed environmental liaison personnel within their organizations to maintain contact with government environmental agencies. This practice facilitates rapid communication between government and an individual industry and helps to ensure that information from the government reaches the proper level of administrative authority within a given plant.[38] In general such coordinating practices reflect a long Swedish tradition of government by consultation and consensus.

Reference Notes

Numbers in brackets following entries are the identification numbers assigned to documents which have been abstracted for the Foreign Exchange Documents Program of the EPA Office of International Activities. Copies of documents are filed under these numbers at the EPA Headquarters Library in Washington, D.C.

1. "June 3, 1976 Royal Ordinance No. 485 on Amendment in the Instruction (1967:444) for the National Environment Protection Board," Svensk författningssamling, (Stockholm: Norstedt, 1976), p. 1.

2. ibid., p. 2.

3. ibid.

4. "June 3, 1976 Royal Ordinance No. 485," op. cit., p. 1.

5. ibid.

6. Sweden, National Environment Protection Board, Naturvårdsverkets årsbok 1973, (Solna: Almänna förlaget, 1974), p. 112. [ID #02305A]

7. ibid.

8. United States, Department of State, "Science and Technology in Sweden - VI - Environment," Department of State Airgram, no. A-87, (Stockholm: Amembassy, March 28, 1975), p. 3. [ID #02762A]

9. Naturvårdsverkets årsbok, op. cit., p. 112.

10. ibid.

11. Sweden, Royal Ministry for Foreign Affairs, Memorandum Concerning Environmental Activities in Sweden. Prepared as a Supplement to Sweden's National Report to the United Nations on the Human Environment, (Stockholm: Royal Ministry for Foreign Affairs, January 3, 1974), p. 17. [ID #01867A]

12. Lars Emmelin, "The Right of Common Access," Current Sweden: Environmental Planning in Sweden, no. 61, (Stockholm: Swedish Institute, March 1975), p. 4.

13. Swedish Institute, "Environment Protection in Sweden," Fact Sheets on Sweden, (Stockholm: Swedish Institute, November 1973), p. 3. [ID #02691A]

14. Lennart J. Lundqvist, "Shaking the Institutions in Sweden," Environment, vol. 16, no. 3, October 1974, p. 28. [ID #02775A]

15. Lennart Persson, "The Environment Protection Act," Environment Protection Act. Marine Dumping Act With Commentaries, (Stockholm: Royal Ministry for Foreign Affairs and Royal Ministry of Agriculture, 1972), p. 45. [ID #00129A]

16. This Ordinance replaces: "The December 13, 1968 Ordinance on Devices to Restrict Emissions From Motor Vehicles," "The May 27, 1970 Ordinance on Amendment of the Ordinance on Devices to Restrict Emissions From Motor Vehicles," and "The October 27, 1972 Ordinance on Amendment of the Ordinance to Restrict Emissions From Motor Vehicles," (Svensk författningssamling: Norstedt, appropriate dates issued pursuant to the repealed "Traffic Code of September 28, 1951," in C. G. Hellquist, comp., Sveriges rikes lag, (Stockholm: Norstedt, 1972), pp. 663-712

17. Sweden, National Environment Protection Board, Report on Water Quality Criteria for Swedish Surface Waters. Summary, Publikation No. 1969: 1E, (Solna: Allmänna förlaget, 1969), pp. 1-6. [ID #02744]

18. ibid., p. 5.

19. ibid., p. 1.

20. Werner Martin and Arthur C. Stern, The Collection, Tabulation, Codification, and Analysis of the World's Air Quality Management Standards, Vol. 1: The Air Quality Management Standards of the World, Other Than Those of Subsidiary Jurisdictions of the United States, (ESE Publication No. 380), (Chapel Hill: Department of Environmental Sciences and Engineering, School of Public Health, University of North Carolina, October 1974), p. 158.

21. "High Sulfur Content Temporarily Allowed in Sweden," Ambio, vol. 3, no. 1, 1974, p. 48.

22. Sweden, Royal Ministry for Foreign Affairs, The Environment Protection Act and Related Legislation, (Stockholm: Royal Ministry for Foreign Affairs, 1973), p. 11.

23. Sweden, National Environment Protection Board, Riktlinjer för luftvård (Guidelines for Air Protection), Publikation No. 1973: 8, (Solna: Allmänna förlaget, 1973), pp. 11-20. [ID #02742A]

24. Sweden, National Environment Protection Board, Riktvärden för luftkvalitet: svaveldioxid och stoft (Standards for Air Quality: Sulfur Dioxide and Particulates), Publikation No. 1976: 8, (Solna: Allmänna förlaget, 1976), pp. 6-7, 19-20. [ID #04086A]

25. Such as those cited in reference notes number 17 and 23.

26. The Environment Protection Act and Related Legislation, op. cit., p. 11.

27. Lennart Persson, op. cit., p. 40.

28. ibid., p. 37.

29. ibid., p. 43.

30. M. Donald Hancock, Sweden. The Politics of Postindustrial Change, (London: The Dryden Press, 1972), p. 158.

31. Lennart Lundqvist, op. cit., p. 30.

32. ibid., p. 34.

33. The Environment Protection Act and Related Legislation, op. cit., p. 14.

34. ibid.

35. Bo Helmerson, "Cooperative Environmental Protection Gives Positive Results," Journal of the Federation of Swedish Industries, Special Issue on Industry and Environment, November 1970, pp. 12-13. [ID #02791A]

36. ibid., p. 13.

37. ibid., p. 12.

38. ibid.

Bibliography

Publications that were of significant value in the preparation of this study and are recommended for those undertaking research on environmental protection in Sweden are listed below.

1. Sweden. <u>National Report to (the) United Nations on the Human Environment</u>. Stockholm: 1972.

2. _____. Royal Ministry for Foreign Affairs. <u>Memorandum Concerning Environmental Activities in Sweden. Prepared as a Supplement to Sweden's National Report to the United Nations on the Human Environment</u>. Stockholm: Royal Ministry for Foreign Affairs, January 3, 1974. [ID #01867A]

3. _____. National Environment Protection Board. <u>Environment Protection in Sweden: Legislation, Administration, Research, Grants</u>. Stockholm: National Environment Protection Board, 1972. [ID #00128A]

4. _____. _____. <u>Naturvårds-verkets årsbok 1973</u>. Stockholm: Allmänna förlaget, 1974. [ID #02305A]

5. _____. Royal Ministry for Foreign Affairs, Royal Ministry of Agriculture, National Environment Protection Board. <u>Environment Protection Act. Marine Dumping Prohibition Act With Commentaries</u>. Stockholm: Norstedt, 1972. [ID #00129A]

6. _____. Royal Ministry for Foreign Affairs. <u>The Environment Protection Act and Related Legislation</u>. Stockholm: Royal Ministry for Foreign Affairs, 1973.

7. _____. National Environment Protection Board. <u>Riktlinjer för luftvård (Guidelines for Air Protection)</u>, Publikation 1973:8. Stockholm: Allmänna förlaget, 1973. [ID #02742A]

8. _____. _____. <u>Råd och anvisningar rörande tillsyn enligt miljöskyddslagen (Advice and Instructions Regarding Supervision According to the Environment Protection Act)</u>, Publikation 1971:3. Stockholm: Allmänna förlaget, 1971. [ID #02776A]

The texts of laws and regulations may be found in:

1. <u>Svensk författningssamling</u>. Stockholm: Norstedt. [Ongoing pub.]

2. <u>Sveriges rikes lag</u>. Stockholm: Norstedt. [Annual]

APPENDIX

ENVIRONMENTAL LAWS AND REGULATIONS
INCLUDED IN THIS REPORT

ID No.*

GENERAL

May 29, 1969 Environment Protection Act, No. 387	00129A
May 29, 1969 Environment Protection Ordinance, No. 388	00129A
December 19, 1958 Public Health Statute	01451A

May 25, 1967 Royal Instruction No. 444 for the National
Environment Protection Board

June 3, 1976 Ordinance No. 485 on Amendment in the Instruction
(1967:444) for the National Environment Protection Board

June 13, 1969 Royal Instruction No. 389 for the National
Franchise Board for Environment Protection

AIR

November 20, 1968 Statutory Regulation No. 551 on Reduction of
Sulfur Content in Fuel Oil   00525A

March 24, 1972 Statutory Regulation No. 70 on Reduction of
Sulfur Content in Fuel Oil   00525B

December 1, 1972 Ordinance No. 596 on Vehicle Exhaust Emissions   03447A

RADIATION

March 14, 1958 Statute on Protection Against Radiation, As Amended 00689A

SOLID WASTE

December 17, 1970 Statute No. 892 on Cleanliness in the Municipalities,
As Amended   00816A

December 13, 1974 Royal Ordinance on Sanitation, As Amended   03452A

December 11, 1964 Law No. 822 for the Protection of Nature,
As Amended   00817A

May 22, 1975 Ordinance No. 346 on Environmentally Dangerous Wastes

---

*These are the identification numbers assigned to documents abstracted for the
Foreign Exchange Documents Program of the EPA Office of International Activities.

May 22, 1975 Automobile Scrapping Law No. 343

May 22, 1975 Automobile Scrapping Ordinance No. 348

TOXIC SUBSTANCES and PESTICIDES

April 27, 1973 Act No. 329 on Products Hazardous to Health and to
the Environment   02699A

April 27, 1973 Ordinance No. 334 on Products Hazardous to Health
and to the Environment   02699A

WATER

The Water Code of June 28, 1918, As Amended   00545A

April 29, 1964 Law To Amend the Water Code   00545B

December 17, 1971 Marine Dumping Prohibition Act, No. 1154   00466A

December 17, 1971 Marine Dumping Prohibition Ordinance, No. 1156

June 2, 1972 Act No. 275 Concerning the Prevention of Water
Pollution From Ships, As Amended   03347A

June 2, 1972 Ordinance No. 278 Concerning Prevention of
Water Pollution From Ships

January 22, 1976 Act No. 6 on Measures Against Water Pollution
From Ships Within the Baltic Area

June 17, 1976 Ordinance No. 573 on Measures Against Water
Pollution From Ships Within the Baltic Area

STATE SUBSIDIES FOR POLLUTION CONTROL

June 13, 1969 Ordinance No. 356 on State Subsidy to Anti-Pollution
Measures in Industry   02739A

June 17, 1974 Royal Regulation Extending Validity of Regulation
(1969:356) on State Subsidy to Anti-Pollution Measures in
Industry With Amendment   02739B

June 2, 1972 Ordinance No. 293 on State Subsidy for Environment
Protection Measures in Agricultural and Gardening Enterprises   02760A

June 2, 1972 Ordinance No. 280 on State Support for Waste Treatment   02761A

April 26, 1968 Ordinance No. 308 on State Subsidy for Wastewater
Purification Works   02741A

CPSIA information can be obtained at www.ICGtesting.com
Printed in the USA
BVOW060145150413

318169BV00007B/101/P